To Dave

With love + affection.

Jules

POCKET PRAYERS
FOR WORK

Other books in the series:

Pocket Celtic Prayers
compiled by Martin Wallace

Pocket Graces
compiled by Pam Robertson

Pocket Prayers
compiled by Christopher Herbert

Pocket Prayers for Children
compiled by Christopher Herbert

Pocket Prayers for Healing and Wholeness
compiled by Trevor Lloyd

Pocket Prayers for Marriage
compiled by Andrew and Pippa Body

Pocket Prayers for Parents
compiled by Hamish and Sue Bruce

Pocket Prayers for Peace and Justice
compiled by Christian Aid

Pocket Prayers for Teachers
David W. Lankshear

Pocket Words of Comfort
compiled by Christopher Herbert

POCKET PRAYERS
FOR WORK

COMPILED BY
MARK GREENE

CHURCH HOUSE
PUBLISHING

Church House Publishing
Church House
Great Smith Street
London SW1P 3NZ
Tel: 020 7898 1451
Fax: 020 7898 1449

ISBN 0 7151 4022 1

Published 2004 by Church House Publishing

Introductions, compilation and individual prayers
© Mark Greene 2004

Cover design by Church House Publishing

Typeset by Vitaset, Paddock Wood, Kent
Printed in England by the University Printing House,
Cambridge

CONTENTS

Introduction   vii

Prayers before work   1

Through the day, through the week   13

Issues facing workers today   30

Biblical reflections   63

Congregational prayers   70

Index of first lines   82

Index of authors and sources   86

Acknowledgements   87

OH, YOU GOTTA GET A GLORY
IN THE WORK YOU DO;
A HALLELUJAH CHORUS
IN THE HEART OF YOU.

PAINT OR TELL A STORY,
SING OR SHOVEL COAL,
BUT YOU GOTTA GET A GLORY,
OR THE JOB LACKS SOUL.

Anon

INTRODUCTION

We spend a great deal of our lives working –
working at home at a whole variety of tasks,
working in factories and fields, in offices and
trucks, working at school as we study, working
in churches, and working for clubs and
volunteer organizations.

And it's meant to be that way. Human
beings were designed by God for purposeful
activity for the benefit of humankind and the
care of creation – for his glory. Of course, work
is not always beneficial to humankind, satisfying
or ecologically friendly. And it is not always well
rewarded. Quite the opposite, particularly if you
take a global perspective. Many people today
feel that they have to work too long and too
hard for too little reward. And some of us
choose to work too long, too hard for great
reward but at terrible cost to our health and
the quality of our relationships with people
and God.

Curiously, given how central work is to
human life, there aren't that many prayers
about work in our prayer books, nor many
songs about it in our hymn-books. More
significantly, there isn't, according to my

research, much praying about work in our churches or indeed in our home groups or cells. This collection is designed to help address that oversight. Most of the prayers aren't written by professional writers but rather by women and men (and two children) writing out of their varied experiences of the joys and frustrations of contemporary working life. As such, the prayers capture something of the diversity of ways in which workers pray – before, during and after work. Some are obviously prayers that we could all use. Others, like the psalms in the Bible, are prayers that indicate a way you might pray and will hopefully act as springboards for your own words.

I have met most of the contributors. Those I haven't met, and who are still alive, I have been introduced to by people I know and trust. And I'm very grateful to them for their contributions. All of them are people who look to God to help them do 'whatever they do' in his strength and for his glory. I hope that their words, and indeed mine, will help you know God's presence, grace and wisdom in whatever you do.

Mark Greene
The London Institute for Contemporary Christianity

PRAYERS BEFORE WORK

How many tasks to do in a day? Ten, twenty, a hundred, a thousand? And all to be done, whatever they are, 'with all your heart, as working for the Lord' (Colossians 3.23, NIV).

And how many people might be involved? Five, fifty, a hundred? And how are they to be treated? 'Love your neighbour as yourself' (Matthew 22.39).

How can we work and love as unto the Lord without Christ's help? For 'apart from me', Jesus says, 'you can do nothing' (John 15.5). At least nothing that brings the Father glory.

How important then to bring what we do to God, and ask him to help us do it for him, so that it will indeed bring him glory.

May God bless your work;
may your labours not be in vain;
may you rejoice to find today
your creator working with you;
and see your work in heaven,
restored to glory in the new creation.

John Lovatt, salesman

5.00 a.m.

I'm tired, Lord
I was tired yesterday
and I'll be tired tomorrow

the duvet is warm
and safe
and ...

5.30 a.m.

I'm tired, Lord
I was tired yesterday
and I'll be tired tomorrow

the duvet is warm
and safe
and now I've got to get up

I know my life's much better than many
I know I'm soft and pampered
but I really am tired

I love you, Lord
thanks for listening
for being there

even when I'm tired
did I tell you I was tired?
Lord ... I'm so tired

Brett Jordan, graphic designer

At the beginning of the day

Help me today, Father, to live a life
    worthy of you –
to seek to bear fruit in every good work,
to grow in the knowledge of God,
to be strengthened with all power,
to have great endurance and patience,
and in all things to give thanks to you.

Helen Parry, lecturer

A prayer for the day

I receive today from you.
I give today to you.
Please be with me and guide me.

Andy Brookes, insurance manager

Create or consume?

Lord, give me today the grace to create
    more than I consume.

John Griffiths, advertising consultant

Prayer at dressing

Bless to me, O God,
my soul and my body;
bless to me, O God,
my belief and my condition.

Bless to me, O God,
my heart and my speech;
and bless to me, O God,
the handling of my hand;
strength and busyness of morning,
habit and temper of modesty,
force and wisdom of thought,
and thine own path, O God of virtues,
till I go to sleep this night,

thine own path, O God of virtues,
till I go to sleep this night.

from Carmina Gadelica

Dress code

Today my suit of Italian wool
will speak as much as my words.
I know what to pull
from my wardrobe, my stock of phrases,
to impress, persuade, win them.
Today I will draw on the skills
I have been taught,
which build on natural gifts;
my genetic inheritance.
I rejoice in the sense
of my history, learning,
voice, the moment, all in tune;
the audience a silent chorus.
Help me, Lord,
to give you pleasure on the days
when everything sings;
to remember you in the small
excellences of my choice of suit,
or phrase; a task well done.

Rosemary Hector, project coordinator NHS and writer

The elixir

Teach me, my God and King,
in all things thee to see,
and what I do in anything
to do it as for thee.

The man that looks on glass
on it may stay his eye,
or if he pleaseth, through it pass
and then the heaven espy.

All may of thee partake;
nothing can be so mean,
which with this tincture, 'for thy sake',
will not grow bright and clean.

A servant with this clause
makes drudgery divine;
who sweeps a room, as for thy laws,
makes that and the action fine.

This is the famous stone
that turneth all to gold;
for that which God doth touch and own
cannot for less be told.

George Herbert

Committing all

All that I am, Lord,
I place into your hands.
All that I do, Lord,
I place into your hands.

Everything I work for,
I place into your hands.
Everything I hope for,
I place into your hands.

The troubles that weary me,
I place into your hands.
Thoughts that disturb me,
I place into your hands.

Each that I pray for,
I place into your hands.
Each that I care for,
I place into your hands.

The Northumbria Community, extract from the Oswald Liturgy

*

Before the day begins

Heavenly Father, may your name
be glorified in our work today.

I lift up to you and ask your blessing
upon each person who works here.

May those who know you be filled with
your presence and strengthened to do their
work according to your will. May they
conduct themselves so that those who do
not yet know you may see your light shine
through them.

May those who do not yet know you
have their blindness to you healed. You
know precisely what each person needs
so I ask that your special favour would
rest upon ... (*use a team or phone list if
you have time*).

Lord, may your hand also be upon each
client who comes through our front door,
and upon each person who phones, writes
or emails.

May your blessing and protection be upon each meeting, letter, email and call in which the team are involved today.

All this we ask in the name of your son Jesus so that your name may be glorified.

Jeremy Harbinson, accountant

A commuter's prayer

I failed to get a seat – again,
too many people on the train.
We're stuck in a tunnel;
everybody's sighing;
we're not moving.
I breathe in –
'Let me know your peace and grace.'
I breathe out –
'And help me share it with the people here.'
Breathe in.
Breathe out.
For the sake of my sanity.
For the sake of your kingdom.

Sheridan James, marketing manager

Company prayer

Lord, we know you are with us today
in this place.

Open our eyes, open our hearts, teach us to
see and feel that we are not alone, that you
are with us in all we do, embracing us with
your love and your care.

We pray for our business, for the partners
and their teams.

We pray for wise management decisions,
for mutual respect, honesty and integrity
in our business at all levels.

We pray especially for our overseas work
and network, Lord: for the influence this
firm is having in places like Belfast, New
York, South Africa and especially in Israel.
Lord, we lift our hopes and fears to Christ,
longing for a world in which violence is at
an end, and pleading for those who have
known nothing but brutality all their lives.
Help us all to work for justice and peace
with integrity and compassion.

Candice Blackwood, lawyer

At school today

Dear Lord, please help me at school today
in all that I work at and do.
Please help me in the games I play
and help me to help the people I know.
Please bless me this day and every day.

Alastair Cotterell, Year 5

✳

Prayer before work

Be in my heart, O Jesus,
   to fix my thoughts on you;
be in my heart, O Jesus,
   to give me sorrow for my sin;
be in my heart, O Jesus,
   to fill me with devotion;
O Jesus, loving God,
   may you never part from me.

Without you, O Jesus,
   my thoughts can never please me;
without you, O Jesus,
   I cannot write or speak;
without you, O Jesus, all I do is useless;
O Jesus, loving God,
   stand before me and behind me.

Saltair

Before work

Forth in thy name, O Lord, I go,
    my daily labour to pursue;
thee, only thee, resolved to know,
    in all I think, or speak, or do.

The task thy wisdom hath assigned
    O let me cheerfully fulfil;
in all my works thy presence find,
    and prove thy good and perfect will.

Preserve me from my calling's snare,
    and hide my simple heart above,
above the thorns of choking care,
    the gilded baits of worldly love.

Thee may I set at my right hand,
    whose eyes my inmost substance see,
and labour on at thy command,
    and offer all my works to thee.

Give me to bear thy easy yoke,
    and every moment watch and pray,
and still to things eternal look,
    and hasten to thy glorious day.

For thee delightfully employ
    whate'er thy bounteous grace hath given,
and run my course with even joy,
    and closely walk with thee to heaven.

Charles Wesley

THROUGH THE DAY, THROUGH THE WEEK

God is never more than a prayer away. And many Christians find ways to pause during their day to acknowledge him, to call on him, to praise him – a quick prayer as the phone rings, a pause for prayer before a meeting, a cry for strength under pressure, a plea for wisdom, a moment of reflection as the computer loads a program, or, like Daniel, the deliberate setting aside of times to connect to God.

Entrance

Lord, as I enter my office now,
please come in with me.
You are the true shepherd,
and the great high priest;
help me, then, to be shepherd and priest
to my team today,
to be you to them today.

Asho Bandaratilleke, reinsurance claims broker

Come, Holy Spirit

Come, Holy Spirit,
Still my heart.
Multiply my humble offering of service,
And glorify your name.

Ross Kendall, webmaster

Logging on

This password is a daily prayer
as I log on.
This word with numbers interspersed
is a reminder of my God
and King, my Word
that was in the beginning,
and remains, shall be.
This password is my point to pause
and pray as I log on.
As I connect,
this password is a daily prayer.

Rosemary Hector, project coordinator NHS and writer

At this desk?

Could I kneel at this desk?
Could this screen be holy ground?
Will this phone rise like incense?
Will this meeting bring you praise?
Can this paper mountain sacrifice
    be consumed by holy fire?

Can this work be worship?
It is strain and pain and burden.
Can I give it back to you
who gave us work to grow
    and grace to fail?

Stephanie Heald, editor

Brrring, brrring

Father, as I talk to this person, give me
    a listening ear and a gracious tongue.

Mark Greene

Preparing for work

For an ancestor, a sculptor in wood

Going with the grain is easy;
the pen slides along the sentence.
Even the pause of the semicolon
curves smoothly with the right tool.
Some words whittle to their shapes
with nothing but time
and application; some resist
expression – the knots remain.
Here in your panelled room I take
the rough-hewn planks of thought
hacked with hurts and misplaced saws
and try to cut, with style or wit
and rub and rub the scars until
the form is something more than words
in shape. But difficult to carve
this wood, these words.

Rosemary Hector, project coordinator NHS and writer

Doing things differently

Dear God, please may we understand
what you're trying to make us do
because sometimes we don't stop and think
that God wants us to do things differently.

Anna-Marie Greene, Year 2

Txt pryr

God, u r d ultimate artst+I pry dat
   wat I cre8 2day,
thrgh my spch, thghts+wiv my hnds
will cntain d luv+beuty
dat u put in2 makin dis earf.
Im ur tool, plz use me2cre8 ur wrks.

Laura Garrett, performing arts student

With patients and staff

Heavenly Father, in our daily work
    with our patients and staff,
help us to be patient and kind,
caring and attentive,
perceptive to their needs,
encourage an atmosphere
    of honesty and trust.

Keep us cheerful and willing,
protect us from stress
and excessive demands
and expectations
and keep us fit and healthy.

Allow your Holy Spirit to work
    through us in all that we do
and remind us always to give you the glory.
In Jesus' name.

Nigel Paget, dentist

*

Silently during meetings

Lord, please guide me and use me.

Jeremy Harbinson, accountant

After the meeting

Lord, if anything we said
    was not in your will,
    please help us forget it.
If anything should have been said
    but was not said,
    please bring it to our minds soon.
If things we said were in your will,
    please make the ideas grow.
We ask this in Jesus' name.

Jeremy Harbinson, accountant

Honouring

May my email be honouring
my memos good
my assessments fair
my figures add up
my presentations humble
my humour gentle
my comments seasoned
my transport work
my boss be pleased.

Andy Brookes, insurance manager

Praying for colleagues: an exercise

*In your mind, picture your day at work,
'walk' through it.
Picture your working and meeting
and conversing with colleagues.
Hold them before God,
and as you think of them, repeat the phrase,
'The love of God be upon you.'*

Andy Brookes, insurance manager

A prayer before meetings and presentations

Lord, let me seek to serve, not to impress.

Andy Brookes, insurance manager

Praise

I praise and thank you, heavenly Father,
for the work that you provide for me to do,
and also for granting me the knowledge
    and the skill to do it.
The knowledge of your approval helps
    and encourages me
even if my labours seem to be unnoticed
    by those around me.
And sometimes, Lord, when I'm tired
    and fed up
and tempted to cut corners,
help me to remember that you have never
    given me less than your best,
so I will not give you less than mine.

Anon, mechanic

Thanksgiving

Father, thank you for:
   a job to do
   resources to use
   people to celebrate
   skills to create.

Thank you for:
   a product to produce
   a service to provide
   a challenge to meet
   people to benefit.

Thank you for:
   a budget to honour
   a boss to please
   a deadline to beat
   a standard to meet.

Thank you for:
   the contribution I have made
   the money I am paid
   the reward of serving Christ
   in all,
      in all,
         in all of this.

Mark Greene

Reflections on the day:
a prayer exercise

*In your mind, picture your day at work,
'walk' through it.
Picture yourself doing your work – actions,
conversations, meetings, emails, breaks.*

*Now focus on one particular incident.
What were your feelings?
What might the quiet voice of God
be saying to you?*

Andy Brookes, insurance manager

Prayer for a pause

Teach us, dear Lord,
to number our days;
that we may apply our hearts unto wisdom.
Oh, satisfy us early with Thy mercy,
that we may rejoice and be glad
    all of our days.

The Northumbria Community, extract from the Midday Office

Lord, I'm bored

Lord, I'm bored.
Help me to get stuck in and do
a good day's work.

Andy Brookes, insurance manager

Thank God it's Monday?

Lord, help me, I've got that low
Monday feeling.
I can't see the point of it all.
People at work seem so dreary,
and I feel the same.
Help me to be *different*, Lord.
Help me to ask how their weekends went,
even if they don't ask me.

Anita Kapila, science teacher

At the end of the day

At the end of the day
here, you remind me,
are some of your performance measures,
nine of the treasures that delight your heart.

On a scale of one to ten
how might I rate myself then?

Love ☐
Joy ☐
Peace ☐
Patience ☐
Kindness ☐
Goodness ☐
Faithfulness ☐
Gentleness ☐
Self-control ☐

What, I wonder, would be a satisfactory score?
Simply one or two points more?
How on your scale
can I do anything but fail?

Christ, have mercy and change me
    from within.
Christ, have mercy and change me
    from within.

Mark Greene

25

Rest

Drop thy still dews of quietness,
till all our strivings cease.
Take from our souls the strain and stress,
and let our ordered lives confess
the beauty of thy peace.

Breathe through the heats of our desire
thy coolness and thy balm.
Let sense be dumb, let flesh retire;
speak through the earthquake,
    wind and fire,
O still small voice of calm.

John Greenleaf Whittier,
from 'Dear Lord and Father of mankind'

A prayer on leaving church

I leave this place of worship,
    to begin my worship
I leave the presence of God,
    to begin to find him
I enter my week, to discover you before me
I enter my workplace,
    to discover you working
I return to this place in a week's time,
    rejoicing in having found you.

Christopher Ramsay, vicar

To live like you

Jesus, I don't know whether you chose
your job as a carpenter. It was probably
something you found yourself doing.
Help me when I feel the same.

I don't know if you did it for the money.
I'd like to believe that sometimes you, like
me, were waiting for your wages to pay
your bills.

I don't know if you lived for the holidays
like me. But this I know, that you lived for
a purpose. I want to live like you.

Christopher Ramsay, vicar

A sensory prayer

Take an object that represents your work. Hold the object tightly in your hands. Then as you pray, release your grip until it lies free in the palms of your hands.

Release me from desire for material gain
Release me from hunger for status
Release me from comparison with others
Release me from love of success
Release me from craving of power
Set me free to enjoy all you give me
Set me free to seek you alone for reward
Set me free secure in your love
Set me free to succeed or to fail
Set me free to serve as did Jesus.

Christopher Ramsay, vicar

*

A 24/7 offertory

On Sunday I bring my last week's pain
on Monday my hope of financial gain
on Tuesday I bring my colleague's sad news
on Wednesday I bring my weekly blues
on Thursday I bring the buzz of creating
on Friday for 5 o'clock I'm waiting
on Saturday I sit and enjoy a survey
of all your hands and mine have made
    each day.

Christopher Ramsay, vicar

Monday to Friday

Monday, oh, how depressing.
Tuesday, I'm over the worst.
Wednesday, ½ way through the week,
    that's great:
    tomorrow I'll be saying,
      'It's Friday tomorrow.'
Thursday, nearly there.
Friday, hooray! It's the weekend.
It's Monday again, that's not good.
Lord, you can't want me to live like this,
    racing through the days.
Each day matters to you.
Help me to savour each day as it comes,
    to live for you in the moment.

Anita Kapila, science teacher

*

ISSUES FACING WORKERS TODAY

Work raises so many issues and so many emotions – from the uncertainties and anxieties of looking for work to the often mixed emotions of retirement; from the joy of working with good colleagues to the myriad ways in which selfishness can express itself; from fruitful success to futile failure. And all can be brought honestly and directly to the worker God whose carpenter son knew what it was to work with hammer and saw, to negotiate prices, to do what his clients asked – even when he perhaps had better ideas – to meet deadlines, to be tired and to see rather more of his hard-grafted earnings go to imperial tax collectors than was just.

Bored

I'm so bored.
Are you in this?
This bit, it's difficult,
I sweat a bit, it's dangerous.
Oh, this part is disgusting.
You can't be serious.
Are you in this?
Lord, help me to do my job as to you,
and help me not to complain.

Anita Kapila, science teacher

Prayer for people who work with their hands

O Father in heaven, we believe that you
created human beings in your own image
as workers and we know that your Son,
our Lord, worked at Nazareth with his
hands; bless our hands so that they may
create, in partnership with you, useful and
beautiful things for the improvement of
our human life and work, and so glorify
your holy name.

John Lovatt, salesman

Just between you and me

Some things, I know, are better left unsaid,
kept in the privacy of my own head,
but just between you and me, Father,
I would really rather
work for Attila the Hun
than this arrogant, chauvinistic,
manipulative son of a gun,
this bespoke-tailored stranger to the truth,
this sexual predator, this paranoid pursuer
    of his lost youth . . .

'Just between you and me,'
    the Father began . . .

. . . this incompetent, self-centred,
self-vaunting idolator of the great God I,
snuffling for gold like a pig in a sty.

'Just between you and me,' the Father said,
'ponder this memo in the privacy of
    your head:

One:
    when all you have to say is said
    and some of the things

you are meant to have done
are actually done,
note this: it is me that you work for,
not that son of a gun.

Two:
all your charges may well be true,
but do you really think I love him
any less than you?'

Mark Greene

A good boss, who can find?

My boss is really supportive.
She's a gift from God.
She says the most encouraging things.
I thank you, Lord.
Help me to remember the good stuff,
   when she gets up my nose.

Anita Kapila, science teacher

Ethics

As I thank you, heavenly Father, for all the blessings that I enjoy – for my financial security, for a pension fund, insurance policies and social services – I cry to you for the millions of people who do not even know where today's food will come from.

Forgive us, forgive me, for living so complacently in a world of such injustice and inequality. Create in me the heart of Jesus, for the poor, the homeless, the persecuted, the refugees, the victims of war, those whose children are dying for lack of clean water.

Lord, you created all humans equal, made in your image, and you love us all the same. In every decision I make, every policy I pursue, may I take account of the interests of those whom our society ignores.

Helen Parry, lecturer

Inspiration needed

Great creator God,
maker of all things,
you called forth beauty
    from emptiness
and order
    from chaos.

Is it heretical to ask:
Was it so effortless for you?
Did you struggle, Lord,
to shape the mountain ranges?
Or did you just speak and it was so?

This work you've given me, Lord,
it's supposed to be 'creative'
but so often it is toil, and pain, and struggle.
Sometimes bringing something new to birth
is like trying to blow a boulder uphill
    with a straw –
the effort is exhausting.

Lord, would you help me?
And would the same Spirit that hovered
    over the face of the waters,
that breathed human life into being,
be with me in this work?

Tracey Messenger, commissioning editor

Doing business with God

Dear God, I'm just not sure what to do
    for the best.
Starting this business seemed to be
    the right thing five years ago
but it just isn't working out.
I've met with over a hundred potential clients
and though we don't win them all,
they all tell me that our pitch was the best.
And when we do win new clients
we put so much work into looking after them
that right now it's like walking
    through treacle.

I have never put so much effort
    into something for so little reward.
Now I'm faced with cutting staff,
and running it on my own once again.

What's it all about, Lord?
I want to do what you want me to do
but I have to make decisions
and I haven't heard back from you.
Is this a test?
Is there a pass grade?
Did I take a wrong turn somewhere?
Am I just not listening?

It's been a while since I read my Bible
and I left Job in the middle of a nightmare.
Church just seems like more treacle
and I'm drowning in the stuff as it is.
I love doing things in the community
but I'm working so hard I never seem
   to be there!

How come the things I like doing most
   don't pay the bills?

Thank you for my family
   who put up with me when I'm tired
   and short with them.

Thank you for my friends
   who want to know how I'm doing
   and walk alongside.

Thank you for listening.

Julian Sayer, business owner

Letter from a 24/7 carer

Dear God, please *help*!

I'm finding life very tough at the moment.
My not so good health is incapacitating me
in many areas so I'm feeling frustrated and
insecure. I know this is W.R.O.N.G.

As a lively minded go-getter (albeit a senior
citizen), I'm finding that my present
situation caring 24 x 7 for a chronically
sick and walking wounded husband of
48 years gives me problems. I suppose
I feel trapped.

And I feel guilty when I send him out so
that I can have some head-space, just a bit
of peace, but then I grumble when he's *in*
because I can't get a moment to myself to
be creative, do what I want, cry or even
breathe (I exaggerate but you know).

I badly want to retain my sense of humour,
which diffuses tension, and I desperately
need your assistance in coming to terms
with things as they *are* and not as I want
them to be. Calm in the midst of the storm
and all that!

Thank you, God, for reading this prayer.
I await your kind intervention in these
matters.

Yours sincerely,

Anon

On principle

Thank you, Lord Jesus, that you told us
    that we are the salt of the earth;
that we have an opportunity, wherever
    we are, to arrest corruption and decay.
Help me to do my daily work
    with integrity,
to stand up for truth and justice.
Give me courage to stand on principle,
not with self-righteousness, but with grace
    and humility.
Thank you for the growing awareness
    of ethical issues in business.
Help me to be creative in seeking ways
in which our policies may help the poor
and bring justice to the oppressed,
and help me to encourage my colleagues
    to seek the wider good.

Helen Parry, lecturer

A meditation on having a fit at work

Sitting at the boardroom table
I idly bask in the sunshine pouring through
     the window.
Then as I yawn and glance at my watch,
bells and whistles go off in my head.
I am instantly alert
as if a bucket of cold water has been
     thrown over me.
The others doze on –
can they tell?
They'll know soon enough.

How long do I have?
A minute?
The first wave of confusion arrives,
rolling over the surface of my brain
     like a ripple on treacle.
Where will I fall?
Not on Suzy, please, God.
Not on the boss;
though those thighs would amply break
     my fall.

Please, not an ambulance.
I don't want to be wheeled incontinent
     through Accounts

only to wait on a trolley down the local
until my exhausted legs can bear my weight
and the pain in my scrambled head retreats.

Have I got time to leave the room,
to make it look like 'a comfort break'?
No. The door opens.
I enter the world of the surreal,
staggering drunkenly through the valley
    of shadows
as the world drains of meaning.
I become afraid: very afraid.

I no longer know who I am
or where I am
or who they are
or where the floor is
or what a floor is
wave follows wave of confusion.

I hear someone cry out.
Heads turn.
I fall.
Forget the legislation,
there goes the promotion.

Roy McCloughry, theologian and writer

Hurt

Help me, Lord, to die to myself
and be more alive in you.
Help me to set aside my prejudice and hurts
and be a blessing to others
through the power of your Spirit.
Thank you for your love and grace.

Ross Kendall, webmaster

Isolated

Everyone's talking about me.
I can see it.
When I enter the staff room,
they stop
talking.
They don't even know me.
Help me to give it you.
Oh, help me to be secure in your love.

Anita Kapila, science teacher

Confessions at the kitchen sink

Father, can you see me?

At the sink, weary and wondering what my
life is worth. There's an irritating hymn
that tells me to count my blessings. So I
suppose I should try.

My blessings? My home (in spite of chaos),
my family (in spite of stresses), my health
(in spite of tiredness), my wealth
(comparatively speaking). Well, yes,
comparatively speaking, when I think of the
grinding poverty of so many in your world,
I am indeed so blessed. What else? My
position as your adopted child (in spite of
nothing), and your affirmation of my value,
and the value of all that I have to do,
however repetitive, however boring.

Thank you for enriching me with every
spiritual blessing in Christ, and for
funnelling those blessings down to
me at the kitchen sink.

Helen Parry, lecturer

Gossip?

Lord, I want to gossip about her,
tell them what I know,
so I can find out more.
It feels so good.
I'm torn.
Help me to be holy.

Anita Kapila, science teacher

Money

Lord, you created the fabulous wealth of
the earth, and you saw that it was good.
But I recognize in myself the seductive
power of riches, and the tendency towards
greed, covetousness and discontent. Help
me not to be swayed by the possessions,
salaries, bonuses or lifestyles of others,
or to seek to enhance my reputation by
a display of wealth.

Helen Parry, lecturer

Fair pay?

I can't believe she gets paid that much.
She's younger than me and less experienced.
Why is that? Why don't I get paid that much?
And then you say to me,
'Didn't you agree to work for that?'
'Yes,' I reply.
'So be content with your pay,' you say.

Anita Kapila, science teacher

*

Not enough?

You told us, Lord Jesus, to pray for our
daily bread. Please answer my prayer.
You know my struggle, the struggle
of my family, to meet our needs and
commitments. I pray that you will lead
us to find the best way of meeting those
needs. Everything on earth belongs to you,
and I trust you, in your own way and in
your own time, to provide for us.

Helen Parry, lecturer

Powerless?

Lord, sometimes it appears that the wrong
people are in power. What can I do?
Son of God, you walked the earth and
few knew who you were, or understood
what you were about, yet you submitted
to the authority that sent you to the cross.
Help me to hold on to the hope that goes
beyond the nine to five, the promotion list,
the bonus scheme, the will of those who
direct my work.

Teach me what to pray for in a situation
that seems impossible. Help me to have the
faith to work to the best of my ability, for
you, and as I work to remember that you
are the God who changes things, the God
who is in control.

Rosemary Hector, project coordinator NHS and writer

Running on empty

Look to the Lord and his strength;
seek his face always (Psalm 105.4, NIV).

Lord, it's Friday morning
and my week's supply of energy
ran out some time yesterday.
I'm running on empty.

Lord, this group before me looks
    so expectant –
they want something from me
    that I don't have.
Lord, please feed them;
please take my small stale crumb
and multiply it;
create from it fresh loaves of warm bread
to satisfy their souls.

And, Lord – may I have some, too?
For I am hungry
and running on empty.

Help me to remember, dear Lord,
on the days when I feel energized and full,
that I need your strength and wisdom
just as much then
as on the days
when I'm running on empty.

Beverley Shepherd, management trainer

Before making someone redundant

Oh God, this man's got a family
    and tonight he'll have no income.
Today he's got self-esteem;
    tonight he'll feel rejected.
He's got colleagues
    and tonight they'll be memories.
Today he's got a pension;
    tonight it will be frozen.

And it was I who chose him to suffer
    this pain.
I'm like Pontius Pilate, wanting to wash
    my hands of the blame.
I had to choose someone God.
    I had to choose.
Forgive me if I've chosen wrong.

Lord, help me to be human
    and not just professional.
Help me to do the best that I can for this man:
the best package, the best outplacement,
    the best advice.
Most of all, Father, help me to give him
    the respect he deserves.

May this man find your direction in his life,
may this painful time turn out for his good,
and for those who kept their jobs,
Lord, free them from the guilt of his going.

When I call him in, Father,
may my mind be clear,
may my heart be compassionate,
may my face show honour,
and may my words be gracious.

Of all the things I do in this job,
    this feels the worst.
One day it may be me.
So, Lord, help me to give this news
in a way that I could receive it;
in a way that honours your name.

Paul Valler, finance and human resources director

On being made redundant

Heavenly Father, thank you that I can talk to you. I'm rebounding from the deep pain of being made redundant.

My feelings and thoughts are all over the place.

I may or may not have seen this coming, but the effect is the same – I feel as though I have been kicked in the stomach by a large and angry stallion. There is real, deep-seated pain at the very core of me – my self-esteem is shot, my sense of my own value lies in small pieces.

Now I know why businesses refer to their people as 'human resources', not 'human assets' – instead of being nurtured, I feel as if I've been used up and spat out by my employer.

So I come to you, first, to acknowledge the pain. Give me the courage to share it with you, and those closest to me. Right now, I really need you as Abba Father to tell you just how much it hurts, knowing that you will be gentle, understanding, and will apply the balm I need to deal with the pain.

Next, I ask that you will help me to channel my anger and anxiety into dealing with the consequences as positively as possible.

I come to you, too, for something that I find very difficult to ask. My mind is full of guilty questions. Could I have performed better in the job? Was it my fault? Please show me if there is anything for which I need to ask forgiveness.

And I come to you to seek your guidance on the difficult journey ahead. Help me and my family to cope with the upheaval and uncertainties that redundancy has created – materially, emotionally and at the heart of my relationships.

I ask you to make very clear to me what opportunities now lie ahead: is this to be life-changing, career-changing or job-changing? Please guide me to others who will help me in seeking options and choices. Above all, please let your will be known to me.

I ask this in Jesus' precious name.

David Henderson, technology strategy consulting leader

Rest

Creator God, thank you for establishing
the rhythms of work and rest. Thank you,
too, that you know and understand my
circumstances, and the pressures of my life.
Help me both to work and to rest without
stress and without guilt. May your peace
rule in my heart, through your Son,
Jesus, the Prince of Peace.

Helen Parry, lecturer

Stck

There r tmes wen inspiration wnt cum
+d mre I try2wrk or cre8 summit new
d hrder it bcums.
Gd plz tke away d frustration
dat I feel+rplce it wiv peace.
Hlp me2rely on u2fink of new excitin ideas
so tht wen d jobs dun I cn luk bck@it
+c it as summit we bth achieved, hnd in hnd.

Laura Garrett, performing arts student

Self-pity

Father, take away
  my self-pity,
  over-sensitivity,
  victim mentality,
and give me an unoffendable spirit.
For with you we are more than conquerors.

Father, teach me
  your agape love,
  your compassion
  and passion for the lost,
and grant me grace to show grace.
For with you we are more
than we could ever otherwise be.

Asho Bandaratilleke, reinsurance claims broker

Motivation

Search me, O God, and know my heart;
  test me and know my thoughts.
See if there is any wicked way in me,
  and lead me in the way everlasting.

Psalm 139.23,24

Why?

Why am I doing this job? Am I doing it
because I believe in it? Because I feel called
to it? Because of the salary? Because of the
status? Because I am afraid of change?
Am I trying to live out someone else's
dreams and ambitions? A square peg
in a round hole?

Lord of truth, give me clarity, humility and
integrity, to understand myself and my
motives; and courage to face the facts.

And whom am I trying to impress? My boss?
The attractive human being on the next
desk? My bright young colleagues? Myself?

O Lord, you have searched me and you
know me. You know when I sit and when
I rise; you perceive my thoughts from afar.
Purify my heart so that my highest goal will
be to please you, and to bring glory to you.

Helen Parry, lecturer

Useless?

I am not well, Lord.
I cannot work.
Except I hear you whisper,
'Work for me.'
And so I pray
as best I can,
and work with those
I do not know
and cannot see,
who are too fragile
and broken,
too weak to work,
except for you
who are more broken than us all.
Use me, Lord,
though I'm almost use-less.
Use me
and I will rise expectantly
and shame will slip away,
for I have work to do today
which cannot wait.
And so I pray ...

Lynne Chitty, volunteer

My saucepans speak to me of God

My saucepans speak to me of God!
'How can that be?' I hear you say.
'They're nothing but bits of metal
    and plastic
and wood, perhaps, for handles –
yes, that's it, you think of wood
    coming from trees
and trees, so Francis said,
    should praise their Lord.
So maybe wooden handles speak of God.'

No, no, not wooden handles but the whole.
It comes from his creation –
iron or aluminium mined from rocks;
oil to make plastic, spouting
    from the ground
in prodigal richness –
transformed by humankind
following the inventiveness of him
    we worship,
designed and polished to be beautiful,
a joy to hold and serviceable.

My saucepans stand ready,
   clean and shining,
ready to do my will
and that of him who brought me
to this place and to this time.

They cook the food I serve to others,
those given me by God to tend and nurture,
and visitors who turn my mind to Christ:
'Whate'er you do for them, you do for me.'
As bread and wine is taken,
   blessed and given
by one who ministers,
so my saucepans and I minister
to those needing nourishment and love
   and company;
who then go forth in strength and joy
as ministers elsewhere within the world.

So can you still question
why my saucepans speak to me of God?
Rather, go and let your saucepans
   do the same!

Noel Lovatt, housewife

Prayer for the business traveller

Father, as I come to leave my home again
I feel both sadness and a buzz.
Sad to leave my family again.
But part of me switched on to the trip.
Lord, help me to leave with compassion
when part of me just wants to get it over with.

Watch over my loved ones I pray.
Help them to know my love when I'm gone.
Inspire me with ways to show my care.
Help us to experience the impossible –
intimacy at a distance.

Keep me, O God, from temptation.
Gluttony.
Pornography.
Going with the crowd.
All-consuming busyness.
And thinking I am strong enough
    to deal with it all.
Keep me from ignoring you.
Keep me faithful.

In the queues and the noise
    be my inner peace.
In the loneliness
    be my friend.

O God, give me success on this trip.
And make me a light in the world.
Father, I ask your protection.
And may I return from this exile
with some energy and love to give.

(Ezekiel 11.16)

Paul Valler, finance and human resources director

*

Justice?

Thank you, Father, that justice and mercy
    are so important to you.
I pray for those who don't feel truly valued
    at work, because of pay,
or working hours, or the way
    they are treated.
Help them to speak up with courage
    but also courtesy,
with determination but also dignity.
Touch the hearts of their managers
    and colleagues to listen
with open minds and to respond
in ways that are fair to both sides,
and honouring to you.

Brian Ladd, banker

Woman

So God created humankind in his image,
in the image of God he created them;
male and female he created them.'

(Genesis 1.27)

Lord, thank you that when you formed me
    in my mother's womb
you made me a woman.
I'm a woman who works
    in a man's world –
and most days that's fine.
Most days it's fun.
But every now and then ... I notice ...
I notice the professional shell I have
    put around myself
I notice the sharp words I use to shield
    my vulnerability
I notice the desensitizing that protects me
    from hurt
I notice the temptation to hide
    my femininity –
especially when others ignore or devalue
    me as a woman.

Thank you that you see me
thank you that I am precious and honoured
    in your sight

thank you that your oil and wine tenderize
my toughened skin
and you, O Lord Most High, are all
the protection I need.
Thank you that you see and celebrate
your creation – your woman – me!

Today, as I work, help me to remember
and enjoy
the woman you created me to be.

Beverley Shepherd, management trainer

Worse?

I can't believe this is happening.
I feel terrible, the more I pray
the worse I feel.
Are you really in this?
Fill me with your Holy Spirit.
And help me to trust that you are
in this particular situation.

Anita Kapila, science teacher

A spouse's prayer

Father God.
Here again.
It would be good if it didn't always take
    a disaster to keep me on my knees.
But you are merciful.
Would you be merciful to John?
Would you help him to be everything he
    needs to be to get this team through?
Would you protect him from falling over
    the edge of this cliff?

I pray for the team.
Help them, Father God.
Give them the creativity, stamina
    and wisdom
to deliver something that works.
I pray to you who is the creator,
who has the power, strength, authority
    and wisdom.

And whatever the outcome,
may John know the reality
    of your goodness and grace.
And in some way may this percolate
    through to the people he's leading.

For your glory.

Tracy Cotterell, wife

BIBLICAL REFLECTIONS

*The Bible is full of people involved in work
– Adam the gardener, Cain the shepherd,
Abraham the herdsman, Hagar the slave,
Moses the shepherd, Bezalel the craftsman,
Deborah the leader, David the soldier,
Joseph the manager, Daniel the government
administrator, Esther the queen – and the
fishermen, tax collectors, shepherds, soldiers,
slaves, and merchants who fill the pages of
the New Testament. Their situations and
their responses continue to guide and caution
us today.*

*And the Bible is full of wisdom for work – not
only in the stories but in Proverbs and Psalms
and Ecclesiastes and in the teaching of Jesus,
Paul, Peter and John.*

*As we read the Bible, let us pray that we may
see how God's word applies to our work.*

Mercy

*'Blessed are the merciful, for they will receive
mercy.' (Matthew 5.7)*

Father, you know
that mercy and keeping to tight budgets
    don't always walk hand-in-hand;
that mercy and competition for promotion
    can be uneasy bedfellows;
that mercy and downsizing
    sometimes seem poles apart.

Lord, you who are merciful,
show me how to be merciful
    to my workmates,
    my boss, my clients,
    and those who work for me ...
In all my thoughts about them,
    even when they have wronged
        or annoyed me,
    make me generous.
In all my speech and conversation,
    with them and about them,
    keep me from hypocrisy, harshness
        and unfairness.

In all my daily tasks, and in the decisions
   I'm involved in that may impact many,
  make me careful and considerate.

Give me the courage to show mercy at work,
  even though it may go against
   my workplace culture
or may not be shown to me in return.
Help me to trust you for your blessing in this.

Lord, may mercy fill my workplace,
that we might all receive mercy
   from each other
and from you.
In Jesus' name.

Anne Messer, lawyer and editor

Purity of heart

'Blessed are the pure in heart, for they will see God.' (Matthew 5.8)

Father, make me pure in heart at work,
amidst the deadlines and the ambitions
   and the rivalries.

A pure heart is a strong
   and courageous heart,
  for you have overcome the world.
A pure heart is an enlightened heart,
  for you have called us to a great hope.
A pure heart is sincere,
  for you reward faith with deep assurance.
A pure heart is a protected heart,
  for there your Spirit dwells as a deposit.
A pure heart reveals Christ's own heart
   for others,
  for out of the overflow of the heart
  the mouth speaks.

Amidst the deadlines and the ambitions
   and the rivalries,
Father, make me pure in heart at work.

Anne Messer, lawyer and editor

Praise be to the Lord

Praise be to the Lord, my rock,
   who trained my hands for this work
   my brain for these tasks.
Praise be to the Lord, my guide,
   who gave me wisdom for this decision
   and insight for this plan.
Praise be to the Lord God, my shepherd,
   who protected us from my weaknesses
   and resourced us beyond my planning.
Praise be to Lord God, my strength,
   who gave it when I did not have enough
   who gave it when I had none.
Praise be to the Lord.

Mark Greene,
after Psalm 144.1; 2 Samuel 22.29-37

Who then is my neighbour?

Who then, Lord, is my neighbour?
For whom would I do some
time-consuming favour?
Spend money earned from my not exactly
arduous labour?

Is my neighbour so obviously abused?
Do all wounds that need healing
show a bruise?
Need it be something that makes
the ten o'clock news?

Who then is my neighbour?
I who rarely enter a danger zone
or pass a stranger bleeding on their own.
Are there people I leave for dead:
co-workers with griefs obvious
to the eye but left unsaid,
spouses who, you can tell, sleep chill
in their bed,
middle-aged men, waiting for the cull
that takes their head?

Are there people for whom no tears of mine
are shed:
new recruits whose golden zeal
has dulled to lead,

60-hour-a-week cleaners whose kids
   are not fully fed,
battered bosses trumpeting hope,
   but living in dread?

Help me see, Lord, my neighbours
   as you see.
Help me love, Lord, as you have loved me.

Mark Greene

For such a time as this

Here I am, Lord,
surely the wrong person
  in the wrong place
    at the wrong time.

But apparently your person,
  in your place
    for such a time as this.

Give me Esther's wisdom to see
   a way forward
  and Esther's courage to take it.

Mark Greene

CONGREGATIONAL PRAYERS

'Six days shall you work,' God commands. How appropriate, then, to pray together when we meet together in our churches, for our work, our co-workers, and the places and organizations we work in, to encourage one another to do good work, in God's way, for his glory.

Opening prayers

Father, as we come before you today,
we thank you for your grace and blessing
    this week.
We thank you for guiding us
    and prospering us
in all the work and activities
    you have given us to do.
Help us now to honour you
and to bring to you our praise;
for Jesus' sake.

Anon

Lord God, we come together
    because of you, and for you.
From our week at home, work and school,
where you have been working by your Spirit,
we come together into this place
where you promise also to be working
    by your Spirit.

Meet us now, change us, transform us,
help us to be the people
you have called us to be,
wherever you have called us to be
each day in the week to come.

Simon Duan, pastor

Lord, may what we do here this morning,
not only bring you pleasure,
but may it build us up,
equip us to love, honour and serve you
in every area of our lives.

Anon

General prayers

Almighty God, we thank you for the great
    range of occupations
to which you call your people.
Thank you for the numerous workplaces
in which members of our congregation
    are placed, as lights in the darkness.
We are indeed the Church in the world.
Help us to see our workplaces
    as our mission field,
and to understand what a privilege this is.
May we work conscientiously
    and with integrity,
honouring our colleagues,
encouraging those who are insecure,
and sharing their load with those
    who are overburdened.
But give us courage, too, at whatever cost
    to ourselves,
to stand for what is right and just,
with humility and courtesy,
following the example of our
    Lord Jesus Christ.

Helen Parry, lecturer

Almighty and everlasting God,
by whose Spirit the whole body of
    the Church
    is governed and sanctified:
hear our prayer which we offer for all your
    faithful people,
that in their vocation and ministry
they may serve you in holiness and truth
to the glory of your name;
through our Lord and Saviour Jesus Christ.

*Common Worship, from the Collect for
the Fifth Sunday after Trinity*

We pray for all those who, from within
the structures of our churches, support us
and build us up for our ministry at work.
Bless our bishops, priests and deacons
with true knowledge and understanding
    of the world of work
that by their teaching and their counsel
they may touch the hearts of employer
    and employed.
Lord, in you mercy
hear our prayer.

John Lovatt, salesman

We lift ourselves to you, our Father,
in the many places where we shall be
      this week.
We pray for those who are dreading going
      back to work,
for those who have vital decisions to make,
for those who fear for their jobs,
for those who have none,
for those who work all day at home.
May we give thanks to you
      whatever our circumstances,
and know your wisdom and sustaining grace.

Helen Parry, lecturer

Bless employers' federations
and those responsible for pay
      and conditions at work;
give to those employers who are generous
the power and freedom to create wealth.
Lord, in your mercy
hear our prayer.

John Lovatt, salesman

We commit our work to you, O God.
Make us instruments of your grace,
ministers in your service,
and creators in your kingdom.
Help us to serve the needs of others,
to persevere in truth,
to persist in prayer,
and at all times to seek your will;
so that in all our daily work
begun, continued and ended in you,
we may glorify your holy name.
We make this pledge and prayer
in the name of Jesus Christ our Lord.

John Lovatt, salesman

Bless all those who work for trade unions
and all who struggle to ensure fairness
and justice in the workplace;
give them wisdom and strength
to benefit the employer
as well as the employed.
Lord, in your mercy
hear our prayer.

John Lovatt, salesman

Creed

We believe in God above us,
forming stars and giving life,
making products through our fingers,
blessing land and guiding us.

We believe in God beside us,
Jesus, with us as we work,
suffering, dying, rising for us,
Saviour of the world he made.

We believe in God within us,
Holy Spirit, breath of life,
bringing love to all creation,
our companion and our guide.

We believe in God around us,
Father, Son and Paraclete,
Lord of us and Lord of nature,
giving blessing, peace and love.

John Lovatt, salesman

Offertory prayers

Living God, we come with no great gifts
    to offer, we are ordinary people.
Yet what we have, we bring to you
to make your love felt
    in other people's lives.
We offer you our time and our talents
at home, at work and in the marketplace.
Use us fully so that your love may shine
    through us,
and that the light of your kingdom
may illuminate the world.

John Lovatt, salesman

Father God, thank you that you are
    the giver of everything –
    this world, our families, our jobs,
    our talents and personality.
Thank you for the hard work that has
    been done in the earning of this money.
Thank you for blessing that hard work.
Thank you for the hearts of those
    giving this money.
Thank you for the harvest that will result
    from this money.

Anon

Lord, everything we have you have given
    to us:
  money we have worked for
  money we have been given
  money we have inherited.

Thank you for the all the ways in which
    you have provided income for us.

Thank you for the opportunity to give
    back some of what you have given
to further your kingdom work
    through this community.

Use it, we pray, to your glory.

Anon

✳

Our Lord and creator,
in thanks for all the gifts you have given us
and the rewards our work brings to us,
we offer you now ourselves
and our resources
that your work may be done.

Anon

Lord God, we acknowledge your great
    provision for us
    in all aspects of our lives.
We acknowledge the dignity you have
    bestowed on us by giving our daily lives
    eternal purpose and value.

We thank you for this offering,
    the first fruits of our labour
    as your co-workers,
and we ask that you would use it
    for the glory of your name
and the building of your kingdom.
In Jesus' name.

Anon

Closing prayers

Lord, as we leave this service in this place
to go to other service in other places,
may we see that the whole world
    is your sanctuary.
May all our speaking and all our doing
be work for you and worship of you.

Doug Nason, professor of preaching

Loving God, as we go out into the world,
help us to grow into active disciples
    of the Lord Jesus Christ.
Guide us in all we say and do –
at home, at work, at school,
    or wherever you call us –
so that your name may be glorified
and your kingdom brought nearer.

John Goddard, honorary curate

Lord God of all things, thank you
    that the whole world is yours.
Please help us go out into your world
    to honour you
in our work and our study,
our families and our friendships,
our leisure and our rest.
May our whole lives be made up of faithful
    service for you.

Anon

A blessing

May God bless your work,
may your labours not be in vain;
may you rejoice to find today
your creator working with you;
and see your work in heaven
restored to glory in the new creation.
And the blessing of God almighty, the
Father, the Son and the Holy Spirit
rest on you and the people working
    with you,
this week and all your life together.

John Lovatt, salesman

INDEX OF FIRST LINES

All that I am, Lord, 7
Almighty and everlasting God, 73
Almighty God, we thank you for the great, 72
As I thank you, heavenly Father, 34
At the end of the day, 25

Be in my heart, O Jesus, 11
Bless all those who work for trade unions, 75
Bless employers' federations, 74
Bless to me, O God, 4

Come, Holy Spirit, 14
Could I kneel at this desk, 15
Creator God, thank you for establishing, 52

Dear God, I'm just not sure, 36
Dear God, please *help*, 38
Dear God, please may we understand, 17
Dear Lord, please help me at school today, 11
Drop thy still dews of quietness, 26

Everyone's talking about me, 42

Father, as I come to leave my home again, 58
Father, as I talk to this person, 15
Father, as we come before you today, 70
Father, can you see me, 43
Father God, 62
Father God, thank you that you are, 77
Father, make me pure in heart at work, 66
Father, take away, 53
Father, thank you for, 22

Father, you know, 64
Forth in thy name, O Lord, 12

God, u r d ultimate, 17
Going with the grain is easy, 16
Great creator God, 35

Heavenly Father, may your name, 8
Heavenly Father, in our daily work, 18
Heavenly Father, thank you that I can talk to you, 50
Help me, Lord, to die to myself, 42
Help me today, Father, to live a life, 3
Here I am, Lord, 69

I am not well, Lord, 55
I can't believe she gets paid that much, 45
I can't believe this is happening, 61
I failed to get a seat – again, 9
I leave this place of worship, 27
I praise and thank you, heavenly Father, 21
I receive today from you, 3
I'm so bored, 31
I'm tired, Lord, 2
In your mind, picture your day at work, 20, 23

Jesus, I don't know whether you chose, 27

Living God, we come with no great gifts, 77
Lord, as I enter my office now, 13
Lord, as we leave this service in this place, 80
Lord, everything we have you have given, 78
Lord, give me today, 3
Lord God of all things, thank you, 81
Lord God, we acknowledge your great, 79
Lord God, we come together, 71
Lord, help me, I've got that low, 24

Lord, I want to gossip about her, 44
Lord, if anything we said, 19
Lord, I'm bored, 24
Lord, it's Friday morning, 47
Lord, let me seek to serve, 21
Lord, may what we do here this morning, 71
Lord, please guide me, 19
Lord, sometimes it appears, 46
Lord, thank you that when you formed me, 60
Lord, we know you are with us today, 10
Lord, you created the fabulous wealth, 44
Loving God, as we go out into the world, 80

May God bless your work, 1
May God bless your work, 81
May my email be honouring, 20
Monday, oh, how depressing, 29
My boss is really supportive, 33
My saucepans speak to me of God, 56

O Father in heaven, we believe, 31
Oh God, this man's got a family, 48
Oh, you gotta get a glory, vi
On Sunday I bring my last week's pain, 28
Our Lord and creator, 78

Praise be to the Lord, my rock, 67

Release me from desire for material gain, 28

Search me, O God, and know my heart, 53
Sitting at the boardroom table, 40
Some things, I know, are better left unsaid, 32

Teach me, my God and King, 6
Teach us, dear Lord, 23

Thank you, Father, that justice and mercy, 59
Thank you, Lord Jesus, that you told us, 39
There r tmes wen inspiration wnt cum, 52
This password is a daily prayer, 14
Today, my suit of Italian wool, 5

We believe in God above us, 76
We commit our work to you, O God, 75
We lift ourselves to you, our Father, 74
We pray for all those who, 73
Who then, Lord, is my neighbour, 68
Why am I doing this job, 54

You told us, Lord Jesus, to pray, 45

INDEX OF AUTHORS
AND SOURCES

Anon, vi, 21, 38, 70, 71, 77, 78, 79, 81

Bandaratilleke, Asho, 13, 53
Blackwood, Candice, 10
Brookes, Andy, 3, 20, 21, 23, 24

Carmina Gadelica, 4
Chitty, Lynne, 55
Common Worship, 73
Cotterell, Alastair, 11
Cotterell, Tracy, 62

Duan, Simon, 71

Garrett, Laura, 17, 52
Goddard, John, 80
Greene, Anna-Marie, 17
Greene, Mark, 15, 22, 25, 32, 67, 68, 69
Griffiths, John, 3

Harbinson, Jeremy, 8, 19
Heald, Stephanie, 15
Hector, Rosemary, 5, 14, 16, 46
Henderson, David, 50
Herbert, George, 6

James, Sheridan, 9
Jordan, Brett, 2

Kapila, Anita, 24, 29, 31, 33, 42, 44, 45, 61
Kendall, Ross, 14, 42

Ladd, Brian, 59
Lovatt, John, 1, 31, 73, 74, 75, 76, 77, 81
Lovatt, Noel, 56

McCloughry, Roy, 40
Messenger, Tracey, 35
Messer, Anne, 64, 66

Nason, Doug, 80
Northumbrian Community, The, 7, 23

Paget, Nigel, 18
Parry, Helen, 3, 34, 39, 43, 44, 45, 52, 54, 72, 74
Psalm 139.23,24 (NRSV), 53

Ramsay, Christopher, 27, 28

Saltair, 11
Sayer, Julian, 36
Shepherd, Beverley, 47, 60

Valler, Paul, 48, 58

Wesley, Charles, 12
Whittier, John Greenleaf, 26

ACKNOWLEDGEMENTS

The compiler and publisher gratefully
acknowledge permission to reproduce copyright
material in this anthology. Every effort has been
made to trace owners of copyright material and
the compiler apologizes for any inadvertent
omissions. Full acknowledgement will be
made in future editions.

Extracts from the Holy Bible, New International
Version (NIV) are copyright © 1973, 1978 and
1984 International Bible Society. Used by
permission of Hodder & Stoughton Publishers.
All rights reserved. (pp. 1, 47)
Extracts from the New Revised Standard
Version of the Bible, Anglicized Edition (NRSV):
© 1989, 1995 by the Division of Christian
Education of the National Council of the
Churches of Christ in the United States of
America. All rights reserved. (pp. 1, 53, 60,
64, 66)
The Archbishops' Council of the Church of
England: from the Collect for the Fifth Sunday
after Trinity in *Common Worship: Services and
Prayers for the Church of England* (p. 73).
Extract beginning 'All that I am, Lord' is from
the Oswald Liturgy and extract beginning
'Teach us, dear Lord' is arranged from Psalm 90

by Jim Patterson (originally published by Youth With a Mission in *The Singing Word* it was used in Midday Prayer), are both in Andy Raine and John T. Skinner (compilers), *Celtic Daily Prayer* from the Northumbria Community, originally published by HarperCollins and reproduced by permission of the Northumbria Community (pp. 7, 23).

The prayer beginning 'I am not well, Lord' is copyright © Lynne Chitty and reproduced by permission (p. 55).

The prayer beginning 'Be in my heart, O Jesus' is from *Poems by Saltair* (edited by Pádraig Ó Fiannachta, with English translations by Desmond Forristal) and is reproduced by permission of Columba Press, Dublin (p. 11).

Prayers beginning 'May God bless your work', 'O Father in heaven', 'We pray for all those who', 'Bless employers' federations', 'We commit our work to you', 'Bless all those who work', 'We believe in God', 'Living God' and 'May God bless your work', are copyright © John Lovatt, orginally published by the Industrial Christian Fellowship and reproduced by permission (pp. 1, 31, 73, 74, 75, 76, 77, 81).